I Got Saved! What's Next?

An Introduction to a Christian Life

Adam Butler

bush
PUBLISHING
& associates

COPYRIGHT

Unless otherwise indicated, all Scripture quotations are taken from the New King James Version of the Bible, copyright © 1979, 1980, 1982, Thomas Nelson, Inc., Publishers.

All Scripture quotations marked KJV are taken from the King James Version of the Bible.

I Got Saved! What's Next? An Introduction to a Christian Life

ISBN: 978-1-944566-78-4
eBook: 978-1-944566-80-7
Copyright © 2025 I Got Saved! What's Next? An Introduction to a Christian Life by Adam Butler

Bush Publishing & Associates, LLC books may be ordered everywhere, and on Amazon.com
For further information, please contact:
Bush Publishing & Associates
Tulsa, Oklahoma
www.bushpublishing.com

Printed in the United States of America.
No portion of this book may be used or reproduced by any means: graphic, electronic, or mechanical, including photocopying, recording, taping, or by any information storage retrieval system, without the written permission of the publisher, except in the case of brief quotations embodied in critical articles and reviews.

Dedication

This book is dedicated to my mama. My mom proved Proverbs 22:6 to me.

She never quit praying for me, believing in me, and speaking into me.

It was she who taught me to pray, to hear the voice of God, and to love the word.

Esther Butler was both my spiritual mother and my natural mother, and now she sits with Jesus.

Table of Contents

Dedication v
Introduction ix
The Gospel. 1
Baptism in Water 5
Baptism of the Holy Ghost 9
Serving in the Church 13
Read Your Bible 15
Tithes and Offerings. 17
Praise and Worship 21
Testimonies 23
Never Get Offended. 25
My Story 29
Conclusion 35

Introduction

In this booklet, I want to guide you through some of the fundamental doctrines of Christ (the basics). You have made the most significant decision you will make on this earth. As you continue your journey with God the Father, Son, and Holy Spirit, you will find helpful insights in this book that can strengthen your connection with Him and help you continually experience His love, which has covered and cleansed you.

Living the Christian life is not necessarily easier; however, it is more blessed and peaceful when you follow the ways of the Lord as instructed in the Bible. I pray that you take these introductions to the Bible doctrines seriously and apply them in your life. Additionally, I encourage you to search the Scriptures to deepen your understanding and relationship with your Heavenly Father.

Before you read any further, please pray the following prayer:

Dear Heavenly Father, God of our Lord Jesus Christ, the Father of glory, please give me the spirit of wisdom and revelation in the knowledge of You. Open the eyes of my understanding so that I may know the hope of Your calling on my life, the riches of the glory of Your inheritance in the saints, and the exceeding greatness of Your power toward me who believes, according to the working of Your mighty power which You exerted in Christ when You raised Him from the dead and seated Him at Your right hand in the heavenly places, above all principality, power, might, and dominion, and every name that is named, not only in this age but also in that which is to come. You have put all things under His feet and gave Him to be head over all things to the church, which is His body, the fullness of Him who fills all in all. In Jesus' name, Amen!

1
The Gospel

The Gospel is an amazing thing. Once an individual such as yourself has heard the gospel and recognized the need for a savior, then accepts Jesus Christ into their heart and dedicates themselves to living for him, it causes a supernatural transfer of guilt, anxiety, shame, depression, and feelings of being unloved. These feelings are exchanged for an inward assurance that we are accepted, forgiven, and loved by the one true and living God. Most say it feels like weights have been lifted off their shoulders, or they feel an incredible amount of joy and happiness. This is the new, recreated power that we are promised in the Bible. The scripture references below explain what happens in the life of the new believer.

That if you confess with your mouth the Lord Jesus and

believe in your heart that God has raised Him from the dead, you will be saved. 10 For with the heart one believes unto righteousness, and with the mouth confession is made unto salvation. Romans 10:9-10

Therefore, if anyone is in Christ, he is a new creation; old things have passed away; behold, all things have become new. 2 Corinthians 5:17

How did this happen? How do I share this experience with my friends and family? Allow me to explain.

The Gospel is simple, and it is about the story of humankind and how the creator had to redeem us from our self-destruction. The first account in the bible is creation, and within creation, the story of the first humans is told. These two individuals are Adam and Eve. Adam and Eve had it made. They were in a beautiful garden that was at the perfect temperature all the time. They had fresh fruit and vegetables all year, and Adam's job was to tend to the garden and God's creation. While in heaven, another thing was happening. An angel wanted to be worshiped like God; in short, the angel was kicked out of heaven to the earth. Jesus told his disciples this:

And He said to them, "I saw Satan fall like lightning from heaven. Luke 10:18

Back on the earth where Adam and Eve were, if you have ever heard the story, we understand that the devil possessed a snake and spoke to Eve about breaking the only rule that God had made.

But of the tree of the knowledge of good and evil you shall not eat, for in the day that you eat of it you[a] shall surely die. Genesis 2:17

Eve was tempted because the snake told her she would be like God. She ate the fruit and gave it to her husband, Adam, and they both ate. That is the moment they became separated from God, their heavenly Father, due to their sinful decision to give in to temptation. Immediately, our Heavenly Father created a plan to redeem humanity and provide them with the option to choose life or death, Heaven or Hell. An eternal reward for the decisions they make on earth, whether to accept Jesus Christ as our Lord and Savior and to live a life pursuing a relationship with him, or live unto ourselves and reap an eternal separation from the love of God.

That story is the story of Jesus. He was supernaturally born of a virgin, just like you are regenerated supernaturally and now feel clean inside. Jesus was tempted the same way we all are, yet he never gave in to those impulses and desires. He also took our place for judgment with the Father for disregarding his laws and statutes. If you have seen the movie The Passion of the Christ, you will see it was an agonizing death and quite the price to pay for reconciliation.

The absolutes that one must believe to be saved are these: you believe in your heart that Jesus was born of a virgin, lived a sinless life, died on the cross as a substitute for eternal judgment for you and me, and he rose again from the grave three days after he was crucified and killed.

He now sits at the Father's right hand and will return for his saints one day. We understand this truth from the scriptures, and a couple of scriptural accounts for your understanding are;

He who believes and is baptized will be saved; but he who does not believe will be condemned. Mark 16:16

That if you confess with your mouth the Lord Jesus and believe in your heart that God has raised Him from the dead, you will be saved. Romans 10:9

If you don't confess with your mouth what you believe, you are not saved. It is a powerful confession of faith and declaration in prayer towards your loving Heavenly Father as you accept Jesus Christ as your personal Lord and Savior.

PRAYER:

Dear Heavenly Father, I believe you sent your one and only son, Jesus, to die for me on the cross as a substitute for the penalty of my sinful lifestyle. I believe he rose again on the third day, ascended into heaven, and now sits at your right hand. I confess Jesus Christ as my Lord and Savior and dedicate my life to living for him. Mold me, change me, and let me forever be changed into becoming more like him. Thank you for cleansing me and making me brand new inside. I love you, Lord. In Jesus' name, Amen.

2
Baptism in Water

Once you have accepted Christ as your Lord and Savior, there are topics called Bible doctrines. It is important to dive into this new life. I recommend picking up a copy of Dr. P.C. Nelson's fantastic book on Bible doctrines to help fast-track and explain a few things. Reading the whole Bible in the next few weeks would be impossible, and since this is all new, allow me to introduce a few of these here.

One of these Doctrines is the baptism in water. Jesus was baptized by John the Baptist in the disciples' accounts of his life here on earth. I prefer full submersion as it is an outward sign that you are dead to sin and alive in Christ. Christ showed us this example when he was baptized in the river. Something supernatural happened on the inside when you prayed the prayer of consecration. In addition, showing our faith through our works is a solidifying act. We see this in James 2:18, *But someone will say, 'You have faith, and I have works." Show me your faith without your works, and I will show you my faith by my works.*

We recognized ourselves as people who had sinned and felt ashamed. Jesus washed those sins away, and we feel clean and alive inside. A new creation has been reborn into the kingdom of God. In the natural, we have a burial when something or someone dies, we put them into the ground. You have probably heard the phrase "ashes to ashes, and dust to dust". A baptism in water represents that you were once a sinner and rose again as a new man through Christ. Being submerged under the water, you're burying your old nature and lifestyles; you have been washed in the water of the gospel, the word spoken that convicted your heart towards accepting a relationship with Yahweh (the Hebrew name for your Heavenly Father). This happened through the cross of Jesus Christ. By faith, we come out of the water, showing everyone that we are a new creation in Christ Jesus, old things have passed away, and behold, all things have been made new. That old person has died; we are no longer bound to old habits, behaviors, or character flaws. Greater is He that's in you than he that's in the world! When we are weak, He is strong.

We can call on the name of the Lord when we feel the old nature rising up and be saved! We can boldly say, "No! I buried that old self in the blood of Jesus; and devil, you saw me when I was water baptized, so get away from me, and I rebuke every temptation and old habit that tries to come back!".

Peter, one of the first apostles, told us we must be baptized in water.

Then Peter said to them, "Repent, and let every one of you be baptized in the name of Jesus Christ for the [a] remission of sins; and you shall receive the gift of the Holy Spirit. Acts 2:38

Showing family and friends the profound change and commitment to a life of faith in Christ Jesus is essential. This presents a valuable opportunity to invite loved ones to witness this commitment.

Something supernatural occurs when one publicly solidifies their faith, an experience that must be felt rather than simply explained. Those who have genuinely committed understand the inner strength that comes from being in alignment with their Savior, leading to what the Bible refers to as "blessed assurance."

Only those who have said the sinner's prayer or prayer of commitment are eligible to receive the blessing of baptism.

Therefore, we were buried with Him through baptism into death, that just as Christ was raised from the dead by the glory of the Father, even so we also should walk in newness of life. 5 For if we have been united together in the likeness of His death, certainly we also shall be in the likeness of His resurrection. Romans 6:4-5

We do not believe this is the act that saves an individual;

faith in Jesus did that. This is an outward sign that you identify with his death, burial, and resurrection, and it becomes a part of your testimony.

And baptism, which is a figure [of their deliverance], does now also save you [from inward questionings and fears], not by the removing of outward body filth [bathing], but by [providing you with] the answer of a good and clear conscience (inward cleanness and peace) before God [because you are demonstrating what you believe to be yours] through the resurrection of Jesus Christ. 1 Peter 3:21(AMPC)

If you haven't already, talk to your pastor and ask him to baptize you in water. Set a date, plan a party—you have a new spiritual birthday! Put it on social media and tag me—it's a celebration worth sharing!

3
Baptism of the Holy Ghost

One of the benefits that our Heavenly Father has provided through Christ Jesus is the empowerment of being born of the Spirit. We see that there is an additional upgrade, so to speak, with being filled with the spirit of God. This is known as being filled with the Holy Spirit and speaking in other tongues. When you get so full of God, there is a rumbling in your spirit, and it has to come out. We give voice to this through words that could be considered tongues of angels, as it is a heavenly prayer language. The Bible teaches us that when we pray this way, we are praying with the assistance of the Holy Spirit. When we become burdened about a situation or someone, we can pray this way until we are overwhelmed with peace and know that God has heard us and is moving on our behalf. The Bible encourages us to build ourselves up in our most holy faith, praying in other tongues through the Spirit.

But you, beloved, building yourselves up on your most holy faith, praying in the Holy Spirit. Jude1:20

This is another doctrine and essential baptism for you and me to live an empowered Christian life. The Apostle Paul wrote of his account:

He said unto them, Have ye received the Holy Ghost since ye believed? And they said unto him, We have not so much as heard whether there be any Holy Ghost. And he said unto them, Unto what then were ye baptized? And they said, Unto John's baptism. Then said Paul, John verily baptized with the baptism of repentance, saying unto the people, that they should believe on him which should come after him, that is, on Christ Jesus. When they heard this, they were baptized in the name of the Lord Jesus. And when Paul laid his hands upon them, the Holy Ghost came on them; they spake with tongues and prophesied. Acts 19:2-6 KJV

We see that it is part of the new creation package. Faith comes into play here as our natural mind wants to protect its comfortable state and stay in control. Urges and reasoning have controlled you for so long that it will take a step of faith to begin this new spirit-filled life. A few scriptures that help us understand this are;

That which is born of the flesh is flesh, and that which is born of the Spirit is spirit. John 3:6

Therefore, I make known to you that no one speaking by

the Spirit of God calls Jesus accursed, and no one can say that Jesus is Lord except by the Holy Spirit. I Corinthians 12:3

The Holy Spirit is given to us to lead, guide, protect, teach, and pray with us. You know if you are full because you speak in a heavenly language.

For if I pray in a tongue, my spirit prays, but my understanding is unfruitful. What is the conclusion then? I will pray with the spirit, and I will also pray with the understanding. I will sing with the spirit, and I will also sing with the understanding. I Corinthians 14:14-15

Being filled is easy. It is yielding to the Lord and giving voice to the rumbling inside your spirit. When you get filled, you may only say one or a few words in the spirit; as you yield, you will get more words. This is similar to a small child learning to talk; it is one word at a time, not full sentences immediately. It isn't how many words come out; it is the fact that you are connecting with the Holy Spirit and praying the will of the Father over whatever you are praying about. I emphasize this: it is not a possession of the Holy Spirit. God the Holy Spirit encourages us, and as we yield to his leading, we must use our vocal cords to make the words. We feel silly initially and almost embarrassed as we don't understand what we are saying or know if we are doing it correctly. Let me assure you, if you are yielding to the Holy Spirit, you can not do it incorrectly. The Bible promises that he will lead and guide us to the truth. I recommend praying in the car or shower, so it is a daily practice, and you have an intimate time where there is no distraction. You can't be embarrassed when alone. Also, attend some prayer meetings at church, and you will see a zeal that supersedes emotions.

We do have to overcome insecurities and yield entirely to the Lord. It is imperative that you pray in the Spirit every day. If you start your days out by praying in the spirit, you will see an increase in the wisdom of God in your day-to-day tasks. The reason for this is that, according to the new covenant, the empowerment of the Holy Spirit will make it as if Christ never left the earth but is with you wherever you go, praying with you when you pray for others or yourself. This is essential to overcoming in the life we live on earth. The evil one has no power over a spirit-filled believer and is afraid of them, as they can stop all his plans for destruction in their life and those around them when they are present.

As Scripture says, "Whoever who believes on him will not be put to shame. Romans 10:11

Ask your pastor to lay hands on you to receive if you feel you need assistance in receiving his gift. Once you receive it, you will speak. Again, attend some prayer meetings at your church. Congregational prayer is powerful, and you will start to develop a love for the Lord's ways.

4
Serving in the Church

We must remember that we have been made new, and old things have passed away. We must realize that means we are not returning to the same way of living every day of every week. We have to become an active member of the body of Christ. The first way we do that is by committing to a local church. If possible, I suggest the church you got saved in is the one you should attend. I believe in divine appointments, so I believe you were led there to receive truth and continual support for a life change. God will put a pastor in your life to encourage, teach, and challenge you.

Once you are committed to a church and have that peace in your inner man that passes understanding, you know you need to serve. I recommend that new believers help by becoming ushers and greeters so they can attend the church services, teaching, and preaching of the word. Once you have been there a while, you may be asked, due to your faithfulness, to help in the nursery or kids' ministry. Working in the kids' or youth ministries is a privilege, as more people come to Christ at that time of their lives than at any other time. Of course, there are other areas to consider, such as housekeeping, production, media, etc. Most churches have a ministry of help coordinator or an assistant pastor who handles these things. Find out who they are, and ask where you can get involved and serve.

From whom the whole body, joined and knit together by what every joint supplies, according to the effective working by which every part does its share, causes growth of the body for the edifying of itself in love. Ephesians 4:16

5
Read Your Bible

One of the components to maintaining the peace and the fire you received on the day you received your salvation and began this new life, is reading the scripture daily. Look at this as spiritual food. Consider this: if you can't handle skipping a meal, you shouldn't be able to go to bed without reading the word. The word of God constantly changes us into the person we were created to be. The Word is how we understand what we believe. We can only track and believe what the pastor or minister is saying if it aligns with the Word of God. To receive the promises from God, we read here;

My son, give attention to my words; Incline your ear to my sayings. 21 Do not let them depart from your eyes; Keep them in the midst of your heart; 22 For they are life to those who find them, and health to all their flesh.23 Keep your heart with all diligence, for out of it spring the issues of life. Proverbs 4:20-23

People in the past have been easily deceived by the devil's cunning schemes, using people who look like they are holy to kill, steal, and destroy. If we study the scriptures to show ourselves approved, we won't be deceived. We learn about our Heavenly Father, Jesus Christ, his son, and God the Holy Spirit.

Jesus said:

It is the Spirit who gives life; the flesh profits nothing. The words that I speak to you are spirit, and they are life. John 6:63

Think of a three-legged stool; it cannot sway or topple over. Your three points of grounded contact are prayer, praise, and scripture reading. If you incorporate these into your daily walk with Christ, you will have a stable life.

6
Tithes and Offerings

This topic can seem controversial. Most people struggle with this area, especially in the infancy stages of being born again. They have served money their entire life, until now. Searching the scriptures reveals that money is nothing more than a tool for God to give you to help more people experience the same life change that you have. Financial freedom can only be found in Christ. Jesus warns us about this controlling spirit that wars against the things of God.

No one can serve two masters; for either he will hate the one and love the other, or he will be devoted to the one and despise the other. You cannot serve God and mammon [money, possessions, fame, status, or whatever is valued more than the Lord]. Matthew 6:24 (AMP)

Tithing was established before the Old Testament law

and was brought into the New Testament through Jesus.

For this Melchizedek, king of Salem, priest of the Most High God, who met Abraham returning from the slaughter of the kings and blessed him, 2 to whom also Abraham gave a tenth part of all, first being translated "king of righteousness," and then also king of Salem, meaning "king of peace." Hebrews 7:1-2

Here mortal men receive tithes, but there he receives them, of whom it is witnessed that he lives. Hebrews 7:8

What I have found to be true is that the more I release my anxiety about the future through prayer, the less this concern for not having enough exists. Tithing is ten percent of all our increase, so when money comes in, we take ten percent and give it to the local church where we attend and are being matured or educated in the things of God. Ten percent would be one dollar for every ten dollars. We learn this from the Bible.

Bring all the tithes (the tenth) into the [a]storehouse, so that there may be [b]food in My house, and test Me now in this," says the Lord of hosts, "if I will not open for you the windows of heaven and pour out for you [so great] a blessing until there is no more room to receive it. Malachi 3:10 (AMP)

Some may try to say this is the prosperity gospel. There is no such thing as the prosperity gospel; there is the gospel of Jesus Christ, and the scripture reveals:

Christ has redeemed us from the curse of the law, having become a curse for us (for it is written, "Cursed is everyone who hangs on a tree"), Galatians 3:13

The curse of the law is poverty, sickness, and spiritual death. This is the spirit of mammon we talked about earlier in Matthew 6. You have heard the saying, "Have money, will travel.". Well, if Satan can keep you poor in spirit and stingy in tithes and offerings, he can keep you from the ability to go on any mission trips or family vacations. The Lord will bless those who honor him. The biblical definition of honor is with substance. So offerings are above your tithe and can consist of money or things. It is meeting the needs of the people around you so God can move in their lives, so he can move through them to reach even more people to Christ. The gospel started with an offering.

For God so loved the world that He gave *His only begotten Son, that whoever believes in Him should not perish but have everlasting life.* John 3:16

Jesus encourages us to walk in this opportunity as well.

Give, and it will be given to you: good measure, pressed down, shaken together, and running over will be put into your bosom. For with the same measure that you use, it will be measured back to you. Luke 6:38

Ask your pastor for guidance on this subject and what resources he suggests to help you get a correct heart about money and the gospel. I leave you with this promise from the bible on this topic.

And God is able to make all grace (every favor and [a] earthly blessing) come to you in abundance, so that you may always and under all circumstances and whatever the need [b]be self-sufficient [possessing enough to require no aid or support and furnished in abundance for every good work and charitable donation]. 2 Corinthians 9:8 (AMPC)

7
Praise and Worship

Times of praise and worship are not just for church. It needs to become a part of our daily lives.

But thou art holy, O thou that inhabitest the praises of Israel. Psalm 22:3 (KJV)

A holy thing happens when you begin to sing unto the Lord. Singing is how we can calm our souls and enter God's presence. Praise is known as the highest form of prayer. The Holy Spirit inhabits the praises given to God, our Heavenly Father. We can bring God's glory into our homes as much as we would like by praising him continually with our mouths out of the abundance of our hearts.

Enter into His gates with thanksgiving, and into His courts with praise. Be thankful to Him, and bless His name. Psalm 100:4

Find some Psalms in the Bible and begin to sing. Eventually, you will find yourself singing new songs to the lord out of the abundance of your heart, as you are so full of his new life. Listen to Christian music that glorifies the lord. We have to change our intake so we don't go back to our old ways or be deceived that we can have it both ways; we cannot experience the fullness of God and practice sin. Compromise will only bring regret and struggle in this life. You and I go in the strength of our Lord and have to keep our minds stayed on Him to remain in perfect peace and have confidence in Him. Music is the easiest way to help our soul (mind, will, and emotions) stay in check. The Bible states; Whoever calls on the name of the Lord shall be saved. This is a perpetual action, and if you sing about the enormity and awesomeness of your God daily, you will see that you are stronger emotionally than you have ever been. God cares for our mental health and gives us the strength to overcome trauma and PTSD from our past. He inhabits the praises of his people, and the anointing breaks the yoke of the stronghold from which we want to be freed. Sing songs full of scriptures and declare them over yourself.

Let the word of Christ dwell in you richly in all wisdom, teaching and admonishing one another in psalms and hymns and spiritual songs, singing with grace in your hearts to the Lord. Colossians 3:16

8
Testimonies

And they overcame him by the blood of the Lamb and by the word of their testimony, and they did not love their lives to the death. Revelation 12:11

Your testimonies have to be spoken. The more you proclaim how God is moving in your life, the more you will see him keep moving you into favorable situations. A true testimony is what God has done for you. A testimony is not who you were or what you did before getting saved; that just glorifies the devil and how he had a hold on you. When you tell a testimony, emphasize the God who saved a deceived person headed to hell. Especially with youth and college-age individuals, they sometimes want to have a wild story of their flirtation with the world and sin. This creeps in through a misgiving testimony about drinking, drugs, and so on, as they begin to idolize the pre-saved hardcore persona being presented. Yet they need to know the heartache of living without God and how he has enriched your life since giving your heart to him. When giving a testimony, share the scripture that helped set you free from what was keeping you back from God's best, not experience. I would like to encourage you to do a word study on a bible app of some sort on any word that you identified with and how you can share from this standpoint.

You will see how amazing it is to be used by God to help set more captives free! Here are a few scriptures to encourage you to share the hope that is within you:

For since, in the wisdom of God, the world through wisdom did not know God, it pleased God through the foolishness of the message preached to save those who believe. 1 Corinthians 1:21

He sent His word and healed them, and delivered them from their destructions. Psalm 107:20

Pleasant words are like a honeycomb, Sweetness to the soul and health to the bones. Proverbs 16:24

9
Never Get Offended

I want to leave you with this word of encouragement as you embark on being the best you can be in the body of Christ and winning the world to Jesus Christ. One of the significant hurdles we all have to overcome is offense. We must always listen to the content of every message and conversation with our hearts. We can not choose the tone or attitude when communication is happening. Still, we can ask the Lord to reveal the motives of the heart behind what is being said in the offensive manner in which it is being delivered. If we listen to the content within the message, we can see the blessing that will set us free within the revelation of the scriptures.

A wise preacher once said, " God will not give you personal revelation when he sends a man of God with the message for you." It is by the Holy Spirit that we receive all illumination of scripture. We have a promise that he will lead and guide us into all truth. We must understand that people are all human and are inspired by God's spirit to speak and instruct us. If you remember, growing up, we all had growth pangs, where our bodies ached due to growth and made us uncomfortable, but we just chalked it up to what it was and kept playing sports or hide and seek with our friends. The number one way to ruin your life is to take offense for someone else against the pastor or the church. We have seen so many people lose their salvation and God's favor in their lives because they chose to separate themselves from the garden in which God planted them to grow.

And He Himself gave some to be apostles, some prophets, some evangelists, and some pastors and teachers, 12 for the equipping of the saints for the work of ministry, for the [a]edifying of the body of Christ, 13 till we all come to the unity of the faith and of the knowledge of the Son of God, to a perfect man, to the measure of the stature of the fullness of Christ; 14 that we should no longer be children, tossed to and fro and carried about with every wind of doctrine, by the trickery of men, in the cunning craftiness of deceitful plotting, 15 but, speaking the truth in love, may grow up in all things into Him who is the head—Christ. Ephesians 4:11-15

Allow me to encourage you. Offense will come, and it will be something you will deal with forever. Just know it's there to choke the word and to remove the blessing from your life. Always go to the source of the offense and have a conversation with the heart of understanding and restoration. We are our own worst enemies; we have to overcome the need to be correct and for everyone to know that fact, or the need to correct one another. God sees all, knows all, and wants you to come and pray to him. If you need to "tell on someone", tell their Dad, our Heavenly Father. Scripture says he corrects those whom he loves; rest assured that he will convict the heart of the individual who is trying to cause so much pain in the church. You focus on God and ask him to help you forgive and overlook the wrongs being done to you. Count it as a validation of your worth to the kingdom of heaven that Satan would use someone you love or that you have to work with to try to stop the blessing of God from coming and overtaking you through getting offended. Take authority over the spirit they are yielding to and walk in forgiveness to break the power of the enemy trying to come against you.

Here are a few scriptures to strengthen you:

He who covers and forgives an offense seeks love, but he who repeats or harps on a matter separates even close friends. Proverbs 17:9

Good sense makes a man restrain his anger, and it is his glory to overlook a transgression or an offense. Proverbs 19:11 (AMPC)

If the temper of the ruler rises up against you, do not leave your place [or show a resisting spirit]; for gentleness and calmness prevent or put a stop to great offenses. Ecclesiastes 10:4 (AMPC)

10
My Story

I was born into a home where my parents had just graduated from Bible school in Oklahoma and were moving all over the country to fulfill the will of God for their lives. When I was two years of age, we settled in the state of Pennsylvania. Pittsburgh was where we would live the next 12 years of my life while my parents pastored an inner city church. I was drawn to a show called Gospel Bill, a cowboy show created to share the gospel truths of the Bible with young children. Our church would show episodes and the vacation Bible school curriculum. One Wednesday night, when I was five years old, I received Christ for the first time in my life. I remember walking up front and turning around in awe. Kids were still sitting in their seats, and some were playing and messing around.

The gospel so moved me that it rocked me at age five, and I knew I and everyone else needed a savior. That was the first time I experienced the compassion of God.

Of course, navigating through public school, especially junior high, was an up-and-down time of high and low emotions. I had a great group of kids in the youth group who genuinely loved God, and that support helped me stay saved. Like every young man, I messed up but was quick to repent in my younger days.

At age fourteen, we moved to Stockton, California. Some things happened while I was in school and church in Pittsburgh that made me a little bit harder and began a selfish self-preservation ideology. At fourteen, this was a crazy time. My family was planting a church and trying to adjust to a new culture. I got sucked into attractive temptations and opportunities that were directly opposed to the call of God on my life. I used to say things like, It is my life; I can do what I want. I developed a dislike for people. I didn't like being a pastor's kid.

In the eighties and nineties, gang culture was big, and though I was never in an official gang, I found my people, or those I thought were my forever people. God always had his hand of protection on me, even when I was running from him. I thought my life only affected me, so I began to live a life of disregard for my blood family and their profession. Little did I realize that Satan was using me to try to stop the move of God coming from the church. My actions resulted in three potential felonies and a full-time, non-paid position at a city park for one hundred and twenty hours of community service. I worked there for so long; when I told the director it was my last day, he got concerned and checked the office, hoping I was wrong. I have always found that time goes by faster if I work hard and don't have the attitude to work harder at not working. The only reason I did not go to jail was God's grace. This didn't put me on the straight and narrow, though I learned to be more cautious. It wasn't until I met my now wife that I had a positive person in my life and valued her opinion of me. She wasn't serving God when we met in high school, but she was raised in church like me. God had a plan. Long story short, we had graduated from High School and sat in the back row of my parents' church while a guest speaker was speaking. My now wife and I were arguing; she was wrestling with wanting to go for God, and I wanted to continue living however I felt like. I remember she looked at me and said, "This is what I want." I knew what she meant–I'm going this direction without you. I evaluated everything internally right there in moments, and I realized in my heart that I love her, and if that's what she wants, I can do the Jesus thing in my sleep; it's easier than how I live now. The Holy Spirit used that opportunity to convict my heart, and I walked from the back of the church to the front, with the congregation watching me. Little did I know that I was about to be rocked forever.

Shortly after rededicating my life, I took a business class

at the local community college. I was enjoying it and had a plan to make money, get rich, and finance the gospel. But my spirit was moving, and I was wrestling with the call of God on my life. My mother sensed this and asked if I thought about Bible college. I told her no, but filled out an application just to appease her. I thought I was clever by telling God I'll go if you pay for it. I was okay with paying for a business management/marketing degree, but didn't want to attend Bible school. Well, the lord stepped in once again as a missionary preaching at our church; of course, he was there to share the Gospel and receive an offering for his mission work, yet at the end of the service, without speaking to my father, the missionary declared that the Lord told him I needed to go to Bible school, that an offering was about to be taken up for him, and that the whole offering was to go towards my tuition. He asked if it would be the biggest offering he had ever received from the church.

Enough came in to pay for the first full year of tuition and books. I had opened my mouth and had to be a man of my word. Even in my worst state of well-being, I have never been a liar, and I feel integrity is what a man is made of; he is worthless without it. So, in the fall of nineteen ninety-eight, I went to bible school and left my family and girlfriend in California. Sparing you many details, I knew I couldn't live without my significant other, so I went home at Christmas and proposed with her father's blessing. We were married by that July.

I could keep going, but I wanted to give an account of how God can use anyone if they are willing. I have spent twenty-four years with my wife as I write this book, and I am overjoyed that she is my best friend and first and last spouse in this life. God is first about relationships; remember that as we go through this life together, the closer you are to him, the better your relationships are around you. Here are a few scriptures that helped me understand these facts and keep heartache far from me;

Though one may be overpowered by another, two can withstand him. And a threefold cord is not quickly broken. Ecclesiastes 4:12

Therefore, what God has joined together, let not man separate. Mark 10:9

A man who has friends must himself be friendly, but there is a friend who sticks closer than a brother. Proverbs 18:24

This is My commandment, that you love one another as I have loved you. Greater love has no one than this, than to lay down one's life for his friends. John 15:12-13 (words of Jesus).

Conclusion

I hope this book has helped you. Please find other resources on the subjects that have been introduced in this book. I pray that you fulfill God's will for your life. We are praying for you and believe that God is doing a mighty work inside of you. You are never alone. The Father, Jesus, and the Holy Spirit are ever-present to help and lead you. Apply the truths in this book, and I look forward to hearing the testimonies of your dedication to the service of the Lord!

CONTACT INFORMATION
testimonies@answerschurch.com